RAPID STUDY SKILLS FOR STUDENTS:
HOW TO BE CRITICAL POCKETBOOK

www.How2Become.com

Disclaimer

Every effort has been made to ensure that the information contained within this guide is accurate at the time of publication. How2Become Ltd is not responsible for anyone failing any part of any selection process as a result of the information contained within this guide. How2Become Ltd and their authors cannot accept any responsibility for any errors or omissions within this guide, however caused. No responsibility for loss or damage occasioned by any person acting, or refraining from action, as a result of the material in this publication can be accepted by How2Become Ltd.

The information within this guide does not represent the views of any third-party service or organisation.

CONTENTS

INTRODUCTION

Welcome to *Rapid Skills for Students: How to Be Critical*. In this book, you'll be given the tools, techniques, and advice to become an expert in critical thinking, reading, and writing.

By reading this guide, you'll receive the following:

- An explanation of what critical thinking is, why it's important, why employers value it, and the basics of how to think critically;

- An in-depth look at the formulation and etiquette of arguments, including a dissection of logical fallacies (including examples);

- An examination of the five main critical techniques that you need to learn and be aware of: **inferences**, **assumptions**, **deductions**, **interpretations**, and the **evaluation of arguments**;

- A chapter explaining how to improve your critical style when writing essays.

All of these areas are essential for learning how to become a strong critical thinker, but what is also vital is practice. Make use of the ideas in this book to supplement your own critical thinking exercises, such as attending or participating in debates, reading critical works, and posing your own arguments towards commonly held beliefs.

However, before we can approach any of this, we need to start with a simple question: what is critical thinking?

WHAT IS CRITICAL THINKING?

Have you ever been in a debate with someone about something, and they've said something that sounds dubious? Perhaps they made a claim and failed to provide evidence to support it, or they shot down your argument for reasons that didn't seem relevant or fair. If you picked up on either of these, then you might have 'the eye' (or ear) for critical thinking.

Critical thinking is the activity of studying arguments, the ideas that they're made up of, and the logic that binds them together. When partaking in critical thinking, you're concerned with the structure of arguments, and whether they follow agreed-upon conventions. If an argument follows these rules, then it's usually considered to be a strong argument. However, if an argument sounds suspicious, imprecise, or poorly supported, then you'll need to figure out why and identify it. This is the role of the critical thinker, both during debates and everyday life.

<u>Critical thinkers need to be on the lookout for the following errors made in argument:</u>

1. Logical fallacies, such as appeals to emotion or appeals to authority.

2. Leaps in logic which don't follow from one to another, such as poorly derived inferences, assumptions, or interpretations.

Critical thinking is a valuable skill in any walk of life, and is highly valued by employers as well as throughout your academic career as a student. This is because having critical thinking skills demonstrates that individuals are committed to looking at situations logically, carefully interpreting evidence, and following arguments to the most well-informed conclusion. This is useful in numerous careers and positions. Essentially, any job that is evidence-based will make good use of critical thinking skills. Therefore, it's in your employer's best interests to ensure that candidates are adept at thinking critically.

WHY IS CRITICAL THINKING SO IMPORTANT?

Critical thinking is valuable for a number of reasons, and its exact use to you will depend on your circumstances. For some people, a strong knowledge of critical thinking allows them to construct convincing arguments. After all, if you know what a bad argument sounds and looks like, you'll be able to recognise when your arguments could be stronger, and adjust them adequately. If you wanted to construct a convincing argument for something you believe in, then critical thinking would give you the tools to argue in a way that avoids logical fallacies whilst also being clear and engaging.

Alternatively, critical thinking can be used to pick holes in arguments and beliefs that other people hold. For example, you might know someone who holds many racial prejudices, whilst using recent terrorist attacks as evidence for why his or her thinking is acceptable. You could argue that he or she is 'cherry-picking' evidence that supports their belief, whilst ignoring data that contradicts his or her claim. Therefore, he or she is making an unfair generalisation.

In the modern age of mass information, thanks to the internet, it's possible to be bombarded by news, facts, and opinions. Sadly, not everyone is so concerned with telling the truth as they are with pushing ideological agendas or manipulating people for their own financial gain. This means that you can't believe everything that you read. Not only will critical thinking equip you with knowledge about arguments, fallacies, and other argumentative missteps, but becoming a critical thinker involves gearing your brain up in a way that will make you more aware of good and bad argumentation. So, when you read an article in a newspaper or on the internet, you'll be tuned in to the little argumentative tricks that the writer is using to compel you to agree with them. This means that critical thinking is an excellent tool for those who want to think for themselves rather than just believe what they're told.

What this means is that critical thinking can be applicable to everyday life. You can use it to argue your case, find flaws in other people's arguments, and carefully dissect claims made in the media or other places.

WHY IS CRITICAL THINKING VALUABLE AT AN ACADEMIC LEVEL?

If you're reading this book, it's quite likely that you're a student of a subject which requires critical thinking, such as Philosophy, Politics, Economics, English Literature, or History. At lower levels, such as GCSE (and even A-Level, to an extent), a critical eye isn't necessary; you're usually just telling the examiner what you know.

At higher levels, this changes entirely. No longer are you expected just to *know* details: you'll also need to be able to comment on them in a way that demonstrates a deeper understanding. This will often involve highlighting issues with an argument or concept, but may also require you to examine context and look for the strengths in a piece. In essence, critical reading requires constant *evaluation* of the work that you're studying, then turning that into a critical piece of writing. This is the cornerstone of many university courses, particularly in the Humanities and Arts.

For these subjects, good critical thinking skills aren't merely *useful*, they're *vital*. This means that in order to get the highest grades, you need to have a critical eye for what you're studying. In this book, you'll receive the tools to give you a critical lens for viewing ideas and arguments.

WHY DO EMPLOYERS CARE ABOUT CRITICAL THINKING?

While critical thinking is a great skill to possess in general, some employers also care about candidates being able to demonstrate and use critical thinking skills in a work environment.

<u>Employers like to see critical thinking skills for two reasons:</u>

1. Critical thinking demonstrates high intelligence and self-awareness. Being able to create strong arguments, as well as identify argumentative flaws, is a difficult skill to train properly. Therefore, you need to be intelligent and committed – two traits that employers love to see.

2. Critical thinking is as useful in the workplace as it is in everyday life. In some jobs, critical thinking skills will be necessary to create plans based on evidence, and identify what the problems with current objectives are.

Critical thinking can be used to point out faulty arguments or incorrect ways of thinking that could have a great impact on a business. For example, let's say that you work for a company that's currently doing exceptionally well. Year on year, profits are rising. After three years of this trend, executives might increase bonuses, or expand in ways that would cost a lot of money. Either way, the company will be overspending because they assume that profits will be up once again this year.

This is an example of the 'hot-hand' fallacy – where one assumes that, because they're 'on a roll', they simply can't lose. What if they overspent this year, and then profits happened to fall drastically? Pointing out that they can't be sure that profits will rise, and therefore should exercise caution, could prevent serious damage to the business. Fallacies such as the 'hot-hand' are unknowingly used all the time, even by incredibly intelligent people. Critical thinkers are useful in situations like these because they're more likely to identify flaws in argument and thought processes than those who aren't aware of them.

A critical thinker's mindset has other excellent applications, such as the ability to closely follow a piece of text and highlight issues with it. At school, or perhaps in some job applications, you might have been asked to complete a 'comprehension' task. This involves reading a passage, and then answering questions based on it. The goal here is to test the candidate's ability to pick out key pieces of information when answering questions.

Critical thinking is similar to this as it requires you to pay close attention to a piece of text, or a spoken argument, and extract the most important details. However, critical thinkers go a step further than simply regurgitating facts – they need to get 'behind' these statements, and find out what conditions they're operating under. Are the statements inferences based on data, or are they baseless assumptions? These are the skills that employers find incredibly useful.

HOW CAN I PREPARE TO BE A GOOD CRITICAL THINKER?

In order to be an effective critical thinker, you need to adopt a critical thinker's mindset. This involves a number of different activities and lifestyle changes. We've already discussed reading articles and watching debates; on top of those, there are a few things you can do to make yourself a better critical thinker.

QUESTION YOUR BELIEFS

The first step that you can take at any time is to start questioning things you've been told. You don't have to reject everything you know, but take some time to think about the following questions:

- How do I know that God exists?

- How do I know that I exist?

- How do I know that the sun will rise tomorrow?

- How do I know that the external world that I experience exists?

- How do I know that the fridge light turns off when I shut the door?

- How do I know that two plus two equals four?

To think about these beliefs in such a way is known as scepticism. When thinking about all of the above, you might actually come to reasonable conclusions.

For example, you don't know for certain that the fridge light turns off when the fridge shuts because you can't observe it. However, you can observe pressing the button inside the fridge which turns off the light. You can also observe the shape of the fridge door, and conclude that when it shuts, the inside of the door presses against the button, which turns off the light. Therefore, you can be fairly sure that the light from the fridge goes off when the fridge door shuts.

For other questions, the answer might not come as easily. For instance, the only way you might 'know' that the sun will rise tomorrow is because it's risen every day since the earth came into being. However, just because it's risen every day *so far*, that doesn't guarantee that it must rise tomorrow. This is a form of inductive argument – a generalisation based on previous observations. You might argue that the sun rising every day is a rule or law of nature, but how do we know this? For all we know, it may just be the case that the sun rising every day is a regularity, something that happens every day by chance.

In response to this, one might suggest that while we cannot know for certain that the sun will rise tomorrow, the fact that it has risen for every day in history gives us good reason to. In other words, it's *likely* that the sun will rise tomorrow, even if we don't know it for certain.

It isn't a problem if you don't have adequate answers to these questions. Philosophers have been puzzled by these same topics for thousands of years, so don't feel as though you need to have all of the answers. What's important here is the ability to *question* your beliefs, and get to the heart of why you might believe them. We believe that the sun will rise tomorrow because it always has done. We believe that the external world around us exists because maybe it's a simpler explanation than everything being an illusion.

It's also fine to accept some of these core beliefs, even if they don't always hold up to this kind of scrutiny. Extreme scepticism is an incredibly difficult position to maintain whilst also living one's everyday life, so don't worry about rejecting every belief you've ever held. What's more important is your ability to think critically about what you believe or think you know, even if you still maintain those views afterwards.

READ SOME PHILOSOPHY

Although reading non-fiction of all kinds is helpful when trying to become a critical thinker, reading philosophy can put you a step further. You don't need to cover everything, or even read whole books, but try and expose yourself to philosophical arguments and how they're presented. If you can't seem to get into the original works, try and find some companion books or other secondary sources written about the initial book. This will give you the arguments in a format that's easier to understand.

CONCLUSION

Now you have an idea about what critical thinking is, and why it's such an important skill to have. As previously mentioned, being a good critical thinker requires having a specific mindset, carefully attuned to noticing things that others might not. It also requires a good understanding of how arguments are structured, and the rules which make some arguments better than others. In the next chapter, we will be taking a look at both of these areas by discussing the etiquette of argument.

THE ETIQUETTE OF ARGUMENT

In this chapter, we're going to be taking a look at how arguments work. To do this, we need to look at the following:

Learning how to argue effectively can be useful in your everyday life. You'll be able to identify poor arguments that others make, as well as strengthen your own position while in a debate.

THE RULES OF STRUCTURING AN ARGUMENT

Like almost any discipline, there are rules and conventions when it comes to forming arguments. These conventions have been built upon over centuries of philosophical, political, mathematical, and scientific debate. This means that they vary from queries about the very structure of an argument, all the way to manipulation of statistics to enforce one's own agenda.

Generally speaking, an argument takes the form of one or more **premises**, followed by a **conclusion**. In a sense, the premises are the foundation of an argument, whilst the conclusion is built from it. This means that, if the premises aren't strong, then one might question the strength of the conclusion. Likewise, if the conclusion does not fit the premises (or the conclusion does not **follow** from the premises), then the argument will also be questionable.

<u>Here's an example of a syllogism, one of the most common types of logical argument:</u>

Today is Thursday. It will rain between Wednesday and Friday. Therefore, it will rain today.

This is a kind of logical deduction, which involves two premises and a conclusion. It can be re-written as the following:

> **Premise 1: Today is Thursday.**
>
> **Premise 2: It will rain between Wednesday and Friday.**
>
> ___________________________________
>
> **Conclusion: It will rain today.**

All arguments are built from premises and a conclusion. In this case, we have a logical deduction – the conclusion is derived from the two premises and confined to the information given in the premises.

There are other kinds of argument too, such as inductions. These are the result of premises and a conclusion, but usually contain a generalisation of some kind. For example:

Premise 1: Every time I go outside, I get stung by a wasp.

Conclusion: Therefore, I'll get stung by a wasp next time I go outside.

Inductive arguments assume regularity in events. Here's another inductive argument:

Premise 1: There has never been a day where the sun hasn't risen.

Conclusion: Therefore, the sun will rise tomorrow.

Both of these arguments assume that, based on previous occurrences, the same things will occur again. However, there is no guarantee of this, even if it may seem likely. So, while it's likely that the sun will rise tomorrow, it isn't inevitable.

As you can see, arguments are bound together by rules and conventions. The majority of the rules that we'll be looking at in this chapter fall under the category of fallacies. These take many different forms, so it's important to read each of them carefully.

WHAT ARE FALLACIES?

> <u>There are a few different definitions of a fallacy, such as:</u>
>
> 1. A false belief based on questionable arguments.
>
> 2. Faulty reasoning

While these are slightly different definitions, they both touch on the idea of poor reasoning. In essence, this is what a fallacy is – a case of reasoning which is considered faulty.

Fallacies appear in a number of different ways. Sometimes, the speaker does not realise that they've committed a logical fallacy, and has no intention of deceiving people or subverting reason. In other cases, fallacies are purposefully made to convince people of a position that would be untenable on purely rational grounds. In either case, fallacies need to be identified in order to prevent irrational arguments from being made, or potentially incorrect conclusions from being accepted as facts.

The issue with fallacies is that, despite not pertaining to reason, they can still be incredibly convincing – especially to those who cannot identify them. This is one of the reasons why critical thinkers are valued by employers – they can spot unsound reasoning where others might not. This is vital in some lines of work, such as law and economics, but applies to almost any career where important decisions need to be made.

Whenever a decision needs to be made, there will likely be conflicting opinions regarding the course of action to take. Naturally, this tends to lead to debate. Two or more parties will present their arguments, discuss them, ask questions about each other's position, and hopefully arrive at the best conclusion based on reason and evidence.

However, things don't always go so smoothly. Some people have an aversion to being proven incorrect, and this can result in fallacies being made to make sure that others agree with them. Sometimes, an individual has an agenda that they want to push forward. If this agenda isn't rational, then irrational means might be necessary in order to convince people that it is the correct action to take.

Whatever the case, good critical thinking skills can make the difference between a strong argument being picked as the better one, or a weaker position being forwarded. This can be crucial in some businesses, and is also useful in everyday life.

<u>Fallacies mostly fall under two major categories:</u>

1. **Formal logical fallacies** – an argument with an invalid logical form.

2. **Informal logical fallacies** – an argument which may have a valid logical form, but the premises of the argument do not adequately support the conclusion.

A formal logical fallacy is one in which the conclusion does not necessarily follow from the premises, which are assumed to be correct for the sake of argument. If the leap from premise to conclusion does not follow, then a formal logical fallacy has been committed.

In contrast, an informal logical fallacy occurs when a conclusion may follow from the premises, but the truth or falsehood of the premises themselves is disputable. Therefore, the *premises* of an argument are often the focus when it comes to identifying informal fallacies. Here, we're going to focus on informal logical fallacies.

INFORMAL LOGICAL FALLACIES

As previously mentioned, informal logical fallacies are less concerned with the *structure* of the argument made, and are more focused on its *content*.

One of the most important factors when evaluating an argument's strength is whether it contains logical fallacies or not. While the inclusion of an informal logical fallacy in an argument doesn't make it invalid or false by default, fallacies usually indicate a weaker argument.

The main issue with informal logical fallacies is that, to the uninitiated, they can be incredibly convincing. However, anyone with a grasp on critical thinking and reason should be able to identify and reject fallacious arguments.

Informal fallacies are usually divided into the following categories:

- Fallacies of relevance – this occurs when the evidence provided in the premises of an argument are irrelevant to the conclusion;

- Fallacies of weak induction – the evidence given isn't strong enough to lead to the conclusion;

- Fallacies of ambiguity – the conclusion relies on evidence which isn't present **or** evidence is manipulated either deliberately or accidentally in order to reach the conclusion.

Let's take a look at the most common informal fallacies in these three categories.

FALLACIES OF RELEVANCE

Fallacies of relevance occur when the speaker uses irrelevant evidence in their argument. This can be used in order to get to their conclusion, or to undermine their opponent's argument. For example, *ad hominem* is a fallacy of relevance because it's a personal attack. No matter what the circumstances of the individual making an argument are, what should be attacked is the argument – not the person making it.

The following fallacies are among the most common fallacies of relevance that you'll find in everyday life:

Ad Hominem

This is also known as 'personal attack' or 'argument against the person'. Simply put, this fallacy occurs when the speaker makes comments about their opponent, or uses their opponent's circumstances in order to strengthen their own claim or undermine their opponents. Take a look at the following example:

> *'My opponent knows nothing about the NHS and how it works — he grew up wealthy and has had private healthcare all his life!'*

This argument is fallacious because it presumes that the speaker's opponent cannot know anything about the NHS because they use private healthcare. This might be the case, but isn't necessarily true. For example, the opponent might be a high-ranking NHS doctor, or a government official who is quite knowledgeable about the NHS. So, the circumstances of the individual don't elucidate how strong the argument is.

Moreover, *ad hominem* is fallacious because it doesn't examine the merits of the argument. Consider the following:

Say that an incredibly rich person makes the argument that the NHS is faulty and needs to be replaced with a new system. The response that their opponent might make is that, because the speaker is rich, they haven't experienced what it means to need the NHS. This, of course, is *ad hominem*.

However, what if the exact same argument was made – but instead of a rich speaker, it was a working-class individual who relied on the NHS for healthcare. The argument was the same, but now this *ad hominem* would no longer apply. This is one of the easiest ways to spot a fallacy of this kind.

Ad hominem is one of the most straight-forward fallacies to identify and deal with. Remember that, if an argument attacks the individual rather than the opponent's argument, then it is fallacious. Generally speaking, these arguments are weak.

Appeal to Authority

This fallacy is somewhat similar to *ad hominem* in that it uses an individual's circumstances to strengthen one's position. However, in this case it's the reverse – finding a position of authority to support your argument.

For example, let's say that you're locked in a debate and trying to argue in favour of belief in God. The following would be a fallacious argument:

> *'Belief in God isn't absurd because plenty of intelligent people have also believed in God. Isaac Newton, Charles Darwin, and Albert Einstein all believed in some kind of God. Therefore, we should believe in God.'*

This is an appeal to authority because it uses the example of famous intellectuals in order to support one's own argument. The argument made above assumes that, because Newton, Darwin, and Einstein were intelligent pioneers in Science, they must be correct when it comes to belief in God. However, just because they were intelligent people, this does not mean that they were right about everything.

Here's another example of an appeal to authority:

> *'I know best when it comes to matters about the NHS. I am a doctor, after all.'*

This is an appeal to authority because the speaker is using their own position of authority in order to strengthen their position. Essentially, the speaker is asking the audience to trust whatever they have to say, simply because they're in a position of authority.

This kind of fallacy is usually employed when the individual making the argument needs to convince the audience of something but lacks evidence. To mask this logical leap, the speaker uses their position of authority to speak for itself.

Of course, being an authority on a matter doesn't hurt your argument. However, the way being an authority helps you is that it gives you access to information that others might not. Authority should be used to get better evidence, rather than used in spite of evidence.

Appeals to authority also take the form of irrelevant quotations. Sometimes, a speaker might pull a quote from a famous or likeable individual in order to support their argument, rather than hard evidence.

Appeals to authority are fairly obvious to spot, because they will refer to someone who is held in high-regard, or someone who you can apparently trust.

Appeal to False Authority
Appeal to false authority is similar to a regular appeal to authority, but the 'authority' being relied on is dubious or unreliable. For example, if someone cited a lawyer who had

been disbarred in their argument, this could be considered a false authority.

This can also occur when individuals whose expertise is irrelevant to an argument is cited. For example, if someone cites their favourite musician as an authority when it comes to why you should vote for a specific political party, then this is an appeal to false authority. While this musician might be incredibly talented in their own field, their endorsement of a political party doesn't serve as a strong argument on its own.

Appeal to Emotion

Appeals to emotion are attempts to evoke an emotional response from the opponent or the audience, rather than give evidence for their argument. Take note that it's completely acceptable for an argument to evoke emotion – this is unavoidable in more controversial issues – but the argument cannot *rely* on emotion in order to convince the audience or undermine the opponent.

The following is an example of an appeal to emotion:

'I find it disgusting that there are still people living rough in the UK, don't you?'

The aim of the above question is to put the opponent in a difficult position. If they agree, then they might be compromising their own argument. However, if they disagree, they might come across as callous or even cruel. In a debate with an audience, this could be used to sway the audience in the speaker's favour, rather than convince them using reason.

This is a fallacy of relevance because the emotions of the speaker, opponent and audience are not a valid replacement for evidence and reasoning. The emotional response of any of these parties is irrelevant.

Appeals to emotion are usually easy to identify. If the argument includes an overwhelming amount of emotive language, or questions the emotional status of the audience or opponent, then it might be trying to appeal to emotions rather than make a strong argument.

Appeal to Nature

The appeal to nature is a particularly common fallacy employed when discussing what is right or wrong. An appeal to nature is made when the speaker assumes that something that is natural is necessarily good, correct, or moral. Conversely, the same fallacy is made if one assumes that something that is unnatural is bad, incorrect, or immoral.

Here's an example of an appeal to nature:

'Genetically-modified crops could be a risk to people's health — all those chemicals and modified DNA must be harmful.'

This argument assumes that, because genetically modified crops aren't natural, they must be a threat to people's health. However, there are plenty of things which could be considered natural that are bad.

For example, the venom from a poisonous snake is natural, and it's also natural for the snake to bite prey or potential predators. However, we wouldn't say that it's good to be bitten by a snake, or it's good that the snake injects venomous poison into its victims. We might not say it's bad or wrong either, but either way the status of it

being natural has no impact on whether we think that it's good, correct, or moral.

This argument is sometimes portrayed as 'playing god', especially when it comes to ethical issues such as genetic modification and embryonic screening.

Argument from Incredulity

This fallacy is an appeal to the incredulity of a claim. Essentially, the speaker summarises a point of view, and then comments on how that sounds implausible or unlikely. This can be either personal incredulity, or general incredulity. Here's an example of personal incredulity:

> **'A floating man in the sky who listens to our prayers? That sounds unlikely to me.'**

This is a fallacy because what you personally *feel* about the likelihood of something is irrelevant to the discussion. Your intuitions about how likely something is could be false. Rather, you should be using statistical data which alludes to how likely something is.

This fallacy can be identified by the speaker referring to how probable they believe something to be, without sufficient evidence to prove this likelihood.

Bandwagon Fallacy

This is also referred to as the appeal to popularity or *ad populum*. Fallacies of this kind will make the claim that, since a large group of people do or believe something, then it must be true. Take a look at the following example:

The issue with this fallacy is that it makes the assumption that, because so many people believe in something, then it can't be wrong. However, we know that this isn't always the case. For example, until Nicolaus Copernicus published *On the Revolutions of the Celestial Spheres*, the consensus was that the earth existed at the centre of the universe, and everything else rotated around it. Whether they were intelligent or not, rich or poor, almost everyone in the world would accept that the earth was the centre of the cosmos. However, after the Copernican Revolution happened, this changed. People started to adopt the *heliocentric* model, which suggested that Earth rotated around the Sun.

The central premise of the bandwagon fallacy is that so many people can't be all wrong. However, in the case of

Copernicus' findings, it was the case that almost everyone was incorrect. Therefore, no matter how many people believe something to be true, this alone does not guarantee its truth.

This is a fallacy of relevance because the number of people who believe in something does not serve as evidence. It can easily be identified by the speaker making reference to how many or few people agree with them.

'Fallacy' Fallacy

This fallacy is one which assumes that, because the opponent's argument is fallacious, the conclusion they reach must be incorrect. This is a fallacy because the commitment of a fallacy does not mean that the position you're defending is automatically false. Instead, it just means that the argument presented to defend the position is insufficient.

Here's an example of a 'fallacy' fallacy:

> *'You argue that producing genetically-modified foods is immoral because it will lead us on a slippery slope to genetically modified humans. This is a fallacy. Therefore, it is moral to produce genetically-modified foods.'*

This is a fallacy because the position itself is independent of the speaker arguing for it. It might be the case that a position is incredibly defensible, but has had the misfortune of poor speakers defending it. Therefore, a fallacious argument does not invalidate a position – it merely demonstrates that the argument itself is weak.

FALLACIES OF WEAK INDUCTION

Fallacies of weak induction are those which, while offering some kind of relevant evidence, aren't sufficient to lead to the desired conclusion. This can also include spurious generalisations.

Anecdotal Evidence

Anecdotal evidence is evidence that the speaker has sourced from personal experience. Here's an example of anecdotal evidence:

> *'I'm yet to meet someone who doesn't think that this is ridiculous.'*

In this claim, the speaker is implying that, because they haven't met someone who disagrees on this issue, most people must agree on this issue.

Anecdotal evidence is fallacious because the sample of people that the speaker is fielding isn't necessarily representative of the population. For example, let's say that you're arguing in favour of increasing education on voting and politics. If you made the following argument, you'd be committing the anecdotal evidence fallacy:

The problem with this argument is that the sample of the population you're using to support your argument might not reflect the entire country. It might be the case that most people who don't vote choose not to because they simply don't care. Your sample of the population isn't representative for two reasons:

It's probably too small (polls and surveys gather evidence from thousands of people).

The demographic is probably quite specific since you're asking people you've met. This probably means that the people you've asked share a lot of the same interests, have similar beliefs, or come from around the same area (unless stated otherwise, polls and surveys gather data from a wide range of demographics).

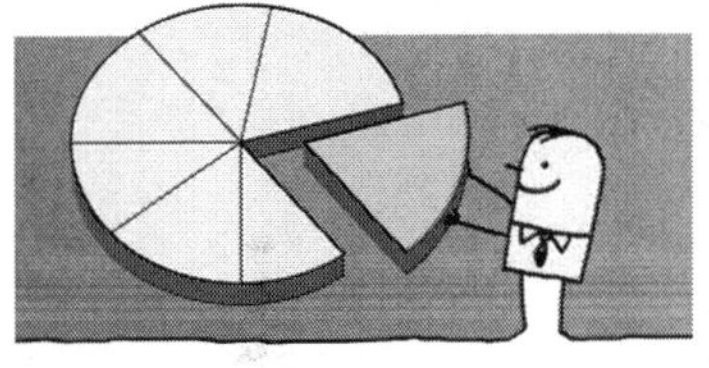

So, this is a fallacy of weak induction because you're making an inductive argument (a generalisation), based on unreliable data. It's fairly easy to identify, since it's usually telegraphed by phrases such as 'from my experience'.

<u>Here's another example of an argument based on anecdotal evidence:</u>

> ***'I've never seen a black swan. Therefore, there is no such thing as a black swan.'***

This is anecdotal since you're basing the inductive argument on your own experience. It might just be the case that you've never been to a place where there are black swans. Therefore, you can't ignore the possibility that black swans exist.

Cherry-Picking/Texas Sharpshooter

This fallacy involves the speaker only picking data which supports their argument, and ignoring evidence which might refute their claim. This is an issue because the speaker's argument isn't being founded on sturdy evidence. When doing critical thinking, one should aim to push the argument which is most well-supported by evidence, data, and reasoning.

This fallacy can be tricky to spot because the speaker usually only displays the evidence that supports their claim. You need to consider as much of the data as possible in order to spot a cherry-picking fallacy – not just the data the person making the argument gives you.

For example, a passage says that unemployment is down but homelessness is up. Then, an argument says that we should continue supporting the current government because unemployment is down, and therefore people are better off. This argument is deliberately ignoring data which doesn't support it. Therefore, it is committing the cherry-picking fallacy.

Correlation Proves Causation

This is a statistical fallacy which assumes that, because there's a correlation between two phenomena, one must be causing the other. For example:

> *'In almost every case, babies grow hair before they grow teeth. Therefore, growth of hair causes teeth to grow.'*

Here, the speaker is correctly recognising a correlation. Generally speaking, babies do grow hair before they grow teeth. However, to say that one causes the other is inaccurate. We can re-write this argument as follows:

Babies grow hair = Phenomenon A

Babies grow teeth = Phenomenon B

Phenomenon A happens in every case that phenomenon B happens.

Phenomenon A occurs before phenomenon B.

Therefore, phenomenon A is the cause of phenomenon B.

This argument overlooks the possibility that there's a cause for both of these phenomena, which explains why there's a correlation between the two. In this case, it's the natural process of growth, which is phenomenon C. This means that, rather than *A causes B, C causes A and B.*

Even if there isn't a clear third cause, it's important not to jump to the conclusion that there's a causal relationship between two or more phenomena. Instead, there might be a hidden third phenomenon which is causing both.

It might even be the case that there is no third cause, and that the correlation is freakish coincidence. This is less likely, but still a reason not to assume a causal relationship between two phenomena.

Whenever an argument makes uses of data in order to reach a conclusion, keep an eye out for what conclusion they're making. If the causal link they're suggesting could be explained by another cause, then they might be committing a false cause fallacy.

Argument from Ignorance

This is the assumption that a claim is true because it is yet to be proven false, or cannot be proven false. Likewise, it is the assumption that a claim is false because it is yet to be proven true, or cannot be proven to be true.

Take a look at the following two examples:

> *'There's no evidence to show that God exists. Therefore, God does not exist.'*

> *'There's no evidence to show that God does not exist. Therefore, God exists.'*

This is a fallacy because, although we don't currently have the evidence to show that something is true or false, this does not automatically mean it is either true or false.

Argument from Silence

An argument from silence is one which reaches a conclusion because there's no evidence against it, rather than evidence to support it. This is a fallacy because, even if there's no evidence that something *isn't* the case, that doesn't automatically mean it is the case. When making a claim, it is vital that you substantiate it. Evidence to refute your claim is only necessary once you've given evidence for your own position.

This is somewhat similar to the burden of proof, where the speaker assumes that their opponent has to provide evidence to prove them wrong, before the speaker has given data to substantiate their own claim.

Here's an example of an argument from silence:

'There's no evidence to show that we <u>do</u> possess free will. Therefore, we <u>do not</u> possess free will.'

Burden of Proof

Technically, the burden of proof is not a fallacy in itself. The burden of proof is a principle that states that whomever is making a claim needs to substantiate it with evidence. It is not the job of the opponent to provide evidence against a claim.

The burden of proof is used fallaciously when the speaker making a claim insists that their opponent proves them wrong. This is similar to the arguments from silence and ignorance, but focuses more on the opponent's ability to present a counterargument to an unsubstantiated claim being made by the speaker.

This is often used fallaciously when the speaker cannot give evidence of their position, but they also know that their opponent cannot give evidence to refute it.

<u>Here's an example of the burden of proof being used fallaciously:</u>

'I might not be able to prove that God <u>does</u> exist, but can you prove that he <u>doesn't</u>?'

When making a claim, it is always the responsibility of the claimant to substantiate their argument with evidence. Until then, the opponent does not have to prove them wrong.

Gambler's Fallacy

The gambler's fallacy is a statistical fallacy which assumes that statistically independent occurrences somehow affect one another. For example, one might believe that they are 'due a win' after a series of losses at a roulette table. However, the amount of times that you've lost at the roulette table doesn't make it more likely that you will win on the next try, since the outcome of one spin doesn't have any effect on the next.

A slightly related fallacy to this is the Hot Hand Fallacy, where one believes that the person participating in the seemingly random activity can influence the outcome.

For example, if you were performing poorly on the roulette table, but your friend was on a winning streak, one might think you'd be better giving your chips to her. However, your friend is no more likely to win than you are – they aren't naturally gifted at winning a completely random game.

No True Scotsman

This fallacy is one which involves moving the goalposts in order to make evidence against one's position invalid. The best way to demonstrate this is with an example:

> *John claimed that no Scotsmen drink wine. Brian, who is a Scotsman, says that he drinks wine. John replies by saying that no* _true_ *Scotsman would drink wine.*

The purpose of this fallacy is to combat legitimate evidence against one's argument by changing the conditions for the evidence. In this quintessential case, John says that 'no *true* Scotsman' would drink wine. However, since no one could agree on what a 'true' Scotsman is, John could exclude any evidence that refutes his argument. This is sometimes referred to as a *self-sealing* argument since it is unfalsifiable. What we mean by unfalsifiable is that, due to the way the argument is formulated, it is impossible to provide evidence against it.

Generally speaking, an argument will not be taken seriously if there is no way of proving it wrong. Creating a self-sealing argument is a way of making your argument unfalsifiable, and therefore is considered to be a fallacious reasoning.

Slippery Slope

The slippery slope is one of the most common fallacies that you'll see in debate, and it's also one of the easiest to identify.

A slippery slope is committed when the speaker assumes that the first relatively small step will inevitably lead to a catastrophic or otherwise undesirable one.

<u>Here's an example of a slippery slope:</u>

'If we promote genetically-modified foods, what's next? Genetically-modified people?'

This is a fallacy because the speaker has no way of demonstrating that producing genetically-modified foods will inevitably lead to genetic engineering. Therefore, this is a fallacy of weak induction. In some cases, this can be considered as an argument from fear, as the speaker might claim that a seemingly harmless step will lead to a terrifying one.

Slippery slopes are usually easy to identify. Sometimes, the speaker even refers to them as 'slippery slopes' in their own argument – which makes them even easier to spot.

A slope is acceptable if the speaker is able to give evidence for *Event A* leading to *Event B*. However, to claim that this is a definite progression from *A* to *B* isn't reasonable since you can prove that future events will definitely happen.

FALLACIES OF AMBIGUITY

A fallacy of ambiguity is a case of faulty reasoning where the speaker has made content of the argument ambiguous. This can include confusing the meanings of words, using an unclear definition to jump to a conclusion, or misrepresentation of arguments.

Argument to Moderation

An argument to moderation is a fallacy which states that the compromised 'middle-ground' between two viewpoints is the correct one by default. While it's quite common for the best answer to exist between two extremes, the problem here is that some people will make the leap to the conclusion that the middle ground is always the best one.

Here's an example of an argument to moderation:

> *James believed that tuition fees for students should remain at £9,000 per year. Ishmael argued that tuition fees should be scrapped entirely, and that a 'graduation tax' should be implemented. Ryan stepped in and highlighted a compromise — that tuition fees should remain at £9,000 <u>and</u> a graduate tax should be implemented.*

Sometimes, a compromise isn't the best answer. The assumption that this fallacy makes is that an extreme viewpoint cannot be correct, and therefore needs to be watered down to suit the middle. Likewise, this kind of argument guesses that the middle ground will suit everyone. However, in the above example, both parties would be unsatisfied with the compromise.

So, while compromise can be a legitimate third-way during debate, the assumption that the middle ground is best by default is fallacious.

Begging the Question

Question begging is a form of fallacious reasoning that requires one to accept the conclusion of an argument in order to accept either one or more of its premises. In essence, this means that the premises are dependent on the conclusion, rather than the other way around.

In an argument, the premises should serve as a foundation for the conclusion to rest on. In a valid deductive argument, this means that if both premises are true, then the conclusion must also be true. The conclusion follows from two premises which are independent from it.

An argument which begs the question is different. Instead, the conclusion is required to be accepted as truth in order for one of the premises to be true.

<u>The following is an extremely common argument which begs the question:</u>

> **Premise 1: The Bible says that God exists.**
>
> **Premise 2: The Bible can be trusted, since it was written by God.**
>
> ---
>
> **Conclusion: Therefore, God exists.**

This argument begs the question in its second premise. Premise 2 argues that the Bible is trustworthy because it was written by God. However, in order to accept this, one must accept that God exists. After all, if God does not exist, then he could not have written the Bible. However, in order to accept premise 2, you have to believe that God exists. Therefore, premise 2 relies on the truth of the conclusion in order for itself to be true. Therefore, it is begging the question.

Question begging is a form of circular reasoning because the argument relies on itself in order to be true, rather than having premises which exist independently of the conclusion. Therefore, it is fallacious.

False Dichotomy

A false dichotomy is a fallacy which assumes that there are only two possible positions in a debate, when in fact there may be more. A quintessential example of this type of fallacy is the phrase 'if you aren't with us, you're against us.' When making this fallacy, the speaker assumes that there are only two positions – both of which are starkly contrasted.

While this might sometimes be the case, the vast majority of debates and issues are more complex than black and white, or good and evil. It's perfectly acceptable for there to be a position which agrees with elements of both sides, or even has nothing in common with either. This argument is a simplification of what could be incredibly complex issues. In turn, this can lead to a straw man argument – where the speaker misinterprets their opponent's view (usually making it look more extreme than it really is).

<u>Here's an example of a false dichotomy:</u>

> *'So, if you're not in favour of scrapping tuition fees, you must think that they are acceptable as they are.'*

This is fallacious because it fails to acknowledge that the opponent might be against the end of tuition fees, but isn't happy with them at their current level. The opponent might not want to remove tuition fees, but instead simply wants to reduce them. This is fallacious because it assumes what the opponent's position is, without considering the possibility of subtlety.

In a sense, the false dichotomy is the opposite of an argument to moderation. Rather than assuming that the middle ground is always best, the false dichotomy assumes that there is no tenable middle ground *at all*.

False Equivalence

False equivalence is a fallacy that makes a comparison between two cases, when in fact the comparison is impossible to make. This can be because the two cases are different in kind (colloquially referred to as being 'apples and oranges'), and in other cases they are so different in scale that a comparison is tenuous at best.

Here's an example of a false equivalence between two cases that are different in kind:

> *'Muslim women conceal their faces in public. Criminals also try to conceal their faces when committing crimes. Therefore, Muslim women are as dangerous as criminals.'*

This is a false equivalence in kind because these two parties conceal their faces for fundamentally different reasons. Muslim women conceal their faces for cultural and religious reasons. Criminals try to hide their faces in order to avoid being identified by witnesses or the police. Therefore, while this might seem to be a legitimate equivalence on the surface, it doesn't hold up under scrutiny.

Here's an example of a false equivalence between two cases that are different in scale:

> *'What with the existence of diversity quotas to fulfil, being a white man in the jobs market is like being a Jewish person in Nazi Germany.'*

The implication here is that white men in the current jobs market are essentially persecuted for their gender and ethnicity, since diversity quotas might mean that companies look instead for women and people from ethnic minorities. In this case, the comparison is made to Jews in Nazi Germany, who were forced into ghettos, worked to death, or killed en masse. While it might be the case that white men are being discriminated against due to the existence of diversity quotas, this comparison isn't acceptable because the difference in severity is too large to be accurate.

This argument is fallacious because it tries to conflate two incomparable cases in order to make a point. This can be used in combination with an appeal to emotion by using emotionally-charged comparisons, such as the Holocaust.

The best way to identify this kind of fallacy is to look at the two cases being compared. If they are different in kind or severity, then the argument is likely committing this fallacy.

Single Cause Fallacy

The single cause fallacy is a form of faulty reasoning that oversimplifies causation so that a phenomenon has either very few or one cause. This is fallacious because it's usually impossible to know exactly how many things are responsible for something to occur. In addition to this, there are lots of causes which might not be easily recognisable, or are so far-removed from the phenomenon that no one thinks to include them.

In other cases, a number of possible causes are identifiable, but the speaker explicitly rejects all but one of them.

<u>Here's an example of a single cause fallacy:</u>

After a school shooting, several different groups demanded for change to prevent another from happening. Some argued that more gun control was necessary, whilst others believed that the issue was to do with how the media glamorises mass murderers. Others opted to blame the parents, whilst the rest believed that the current schooling system was a breeding ground for teenage angst and eventual violence.

This is an example of a single cause fallacy because each of these groups believed that only one of these factors was the cause of the school shooting, when in fact all of these might have played a role. Often, the causes of an event are much more complicated than any single phenomenon. Therefore, it is fallacious to assume that there can only be one cause for a phenomenon.

Straw Man

The straw man is an extremely common form of argument in modern discourse – perhaps somewhat due to social media and people's tendency to only read headlines rather than full articles.

To 'put up a straw man' is to misrepresent your opponent's argument, whether intentionally or not. This can involve oversimplification in order to make the opponent's argument easier to attack, or making the argument look more extreme than it actually is.

<u>Here's an example of a straw man fallacy:</u>

> *Jeff believes that the prison system should focus on rehabilitation of convicts rather than merely punishing them. He argues that, at least in some cases, criminals should be allowed to work whilst serving their sentences, in order to give them the skills they need to reintegrate with society once they've served their sentence. This would be dealt with on a case-by-case basis, and these criminals would not be allowed to work in an environment which required a DBS check — such as working with children.*
>
> *Jeff's opponent, Andrew, says the following:*
>
> *'Jeff wants to let murderers back into work, where they could be a threat to society!'*

This is a misrepresentation of Jeff's argument, since he specifically mentions that this would be dealt with on a case-by-case basis. It's implied from Jeff's argument that those convicted of more extreme crimes, such as murder, would not get this opportunity. Therefore, Andrew is attempting to misrepresent Jeff's argument to make it easier to attack.

CONCLUSION

You now have the necessary tools to identify strong and weak arguments, which will prove useful in everyday life. In the next chapter, we'll be taking a look at different critical techniques and tools that you'll need to understand in order to become an excellent critical thinker.

CRITICAL TECHNIQUES

In this chapter, we're going to be looking at critical thinking techniques that will help you become a better critical thinker. These critical techniques are:

- Inferences;

- Assumptions;

- Deductions;

- Interpretations;

- Evaluation of arguments.

In this chapter, we'll go through each of these five areas, step-by-step. Let's start with inferences.

WHAT ARE INFERENCES?

Inferences are used all the time by people in all sorts of careers. From lawyers and detectives to businesspeople and investors, being able to make accurate inferences to act on is a valuable skill. However, not all inferences are born equal. This means you need to become an expert not only in making strong inferences yourself, but also being able to spot and evaluate the ones that others make.

When someone infers something, or makes an inference, then they are coming to a conclusion which is based on evidence. Logic (whether inductive or deductive) is applied to this evidence, which in turn brings the individual to their conclusion. When someone makes an inference, they're commonly seen as 'reading between the lines', figuring out a conclusion that isn't explicit, but rather implied from the evidence.

Unlike some of the other types of claim, such as assumptions, inferences are based on evidence. However, inferences aren't always correct, and shouldn't be accepted as truth. While an inference might seem correct, it's entirely possible that it's overlooking other possibilities.

It might be the case that you have plenty of evidence for something, but you completely misconstrue it. All of the evidence going into the inference could be strong, but the way you think about it could be incorrect.

For example, you might come across a police officer talking to an individual in the street. You might infer from the fact that the individual isn't in handcuffs, and that the officer is talking to them, that they witnessed or are reporting a crime. This seems to be a sensible conclusion, but there are other possibilities. The individual might know the police officer personally, and is quickly stopping to say hello to them. Alternatively, they might be asking for directions. So, the inference might be incorrect.

Some inferences are better than others. For example, say that you couldn't find your keys and phone. You were sure that you left them on the kitchen table, but now they're gone. You could make several inferences as to how this happened:

1. A burglar snuck into your house undetected and stole them;

2. There was a brief lapse in the laws of the universe and they disappeared into thin air;

3. A ghost took them to play a practical joke on you;

4. Someone else in your house moved them;

5. You are mistaken about where you left your keys and phone, and they're actually somewhere else.

Some of these inferences are more likely than others. For example, you might say that **inference 1** is probably false. This is because it *could* have happened – it isn't impossible – but the chances of it happening are slim. **Inferences 2** and **3** are, depending on your perspective, either probably false or certainly false. This is because you might consider both of these things to be impossible.

Inferences 4 and **5** will fall into the category of probably true. This is because they are the most rational explanations for why your keys and phone appear to have moved from the kitchen table. They don't rely on the supernatural or incredibly unlikely (perhaps even impossible) changes to the fabric of the universe. Whatever the case, they're far more likely to occur than the first three inferences. Therefore, it might be safe to say that these inferences are probably true, and the most likely overall.

You also need to pay attention to whether or not the inference contradicts other information on the topic. For example, say that the text says that people who frequently use social media are more likely to struggle to make friends in real life. If one of the inferences says that social media users are more likely to have more friends, then there's a contradiction between the two. This means that the inference is either probably false, or certainly false.

<u>So, here are the key things to remember when dealing with inferences:</u>

- They're used to derive implicit conclusions from information;

- People often neglect to think of inferences which make more sense than the ones they can think of, leaving them with an inaccurate inference;

- This means that some inferences are better than others; take the time to consider all of the possible explanations for the information you've been given.

WHAT ARE ASSUMPTIONS?

An assumption is a claim that is accepted as the truth without sufficient evidence. These are an issue for critical thinkers because, as a rule, claims made without factual evidence are unhelpful and can be misleading.

For example, imagine if you worked at a company, and the success and survival of it depended on a continued market demand for DVDs. If, at the start of each financial year, executives at the company agreed that DVDs would continue to sell based on zero evidence, this would be an assumption. This could be dangerous since the sales of DVDs could suddenly drop, leaving the company in a difficult position. For this reason, it's important to avoid making assumptions in the working world.

Assumptions are made quite often when constructing arguments. You might have heard the phrase, 'for the sake of the argument, let's assume that...' This is an explicit example of an assumption being made – an assumption that is required in order for the argument to make sense. Of course, you shouldn't leave anything up to assumption when making an argument – even if all parties agree on the truth of the assumption.

<u>So, let's recap the key information about assumptions:</u>

- Assumptions are made when something is accepted as the truth without sufficient evidence;

- Assumptions are usually a poor form of reasoning, so you need to be able to spot when they're being made;

- However, sometimes two participants in a debate will agree on assumptions as a basis to argue from.

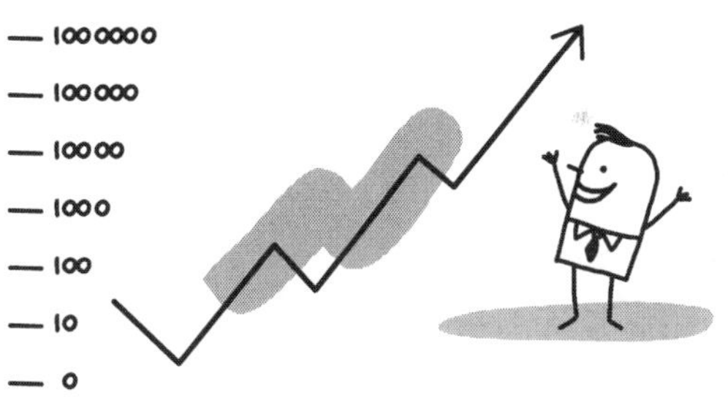

WHAT ARE DEDUCTIONS?

A deduction is a conclusion which is reached logically by examining premises. In fact, a deduction *only* uses its premises in order to reach a conclusion.

<u>Here's a famous example of a logical deduction:</u>

<u>Take a look at the following example:</u>

If all cats have tails, and this creature does not have a tail, then it is not a cat.

This is a deductive argument, and can be simplified into the following premises and conclusion:

Premise 1: All cats have tails.

Premise 2: This creature does not have a tail.

____

Conclusion: This creature is not a cat.

This is a deduction because it only makes use of the knowledge supplied in the premises in order to reach the conclusion. In other words, each step logically follows from the next. It begins with the rule that all cats have tails (assumed for the sake of the argument), followed by an acknowledgement that the creature in question does not possess a tail. By using the powers of deduction, we can conclude that this creature is not a cat, because it does not possess a tail.

In the case of this deduction, possessing a tail is a *necessary* condition for being a cat. In order to be a cat, you must possess a tail. However, this does not mean that you are automatically a cat so long as you have a tail. Dogs, horses, and mice also possess tails, but they are not cats. Therefore, possession of a tail is a *necessary* condition for being a cat, but not a *sufficient* one. In other words, all cats have tails, but not all creatures with tails are cats.

Necessary Condition: A statement is definitely false if it doesn't meet this condition. However, meeting this condition doesn't guarantee truth.

Sufficient Condition: A statement is true if it meets this condition. However, this condition isn't necessary for the statement to be true – which implies that there are other conditions which are sufficient.

If a condition is both *necessary* and *sufficient*, then a deductive statement is true if and only if it meets these requirements.

Let's take a look at another example:

> Premise 1: This shape has three sides and three corners.
>
> Premise 2: If a shape has three sides and three corners, then it is a triangle.
>
> ---
>
> Conclusion: Therefore, this shape is a triangle.

This is a fairly simple deduction which involves a condition that is both necessary and sufficient. In order to be a triangle, a shape must have three sides and three corners. In addition, any shape that has three sides and three

corners *must* be a triangle.

<u>This deduction follows this structure:</u>

P

If P, then Q

Therefore, Q

This is known as a *syllogism* – a form of deduction reasoning that comes to a conclusion based on two or more propositions, or premises. For any deduction, you can enter the relevant premises and conclusion as replacements for P and Q. For this example, P and Q stand for:

P = 'has three sides and three corners'.

Q = 'is a triangle'.

Then, we need to add our quantifiers. For the sake of this exercise, we're going to use *x* – which in this case means 'this shape'.

In logical notation, this then becomes:

Px

If Px, then Qx
____

Therefore, Qx

This translates back to:

This shape has three sides and three corners.

If this shape has three sides and three corners, then this shape is a triangle.
____

Therefore, this shape is a triangle.

We can see that logical notation is a good way of examining how an argument flows. From here, we can get an idea of how the premises relate to the conclusion, such as whether they contradict one another.

<u>Let's summarise logical deductions:</u>

Logical deductions often appear in the form of syllogisms, where the truth of premises leads to the truth of its conclusion;

A deduction is *only* logically invalid if **both** of the **premises** are **true** whilst the **conclusion** is **false**;

Deductions often involve **necessary** and **sufficient** conditions. A sufficient condition means that X has met the sufficient requirements to be Z, whilst a necessary condition means that without Y, X will **never** be Z.

WHAT ARE INTERPRETATIONS?

An interpretation is a conclusion made from carefully evaluating data, and figuring out what information logically follows from it. We make interpretations every day when going about our lives. For example, if you walk into a supermarket and see a '3 for 2' offer on fruit, you can make the interpretation that this offer will apply to apples, bananas, and pears, whilst also conclude that it will not cover broccoli.

Interpretations are similar to inferences, but focus on whether a conclusion logically follows from a statement, rather than what conclusions are *likely* to follow from a statement. Here, critical thinkers are *interpreting* statements to reveal logically sound information. For example, if it's made clear that there can only be white and black swans in the world, an interpretation of this statement would be that there's no such thing as a green swan.

In this sense, interpretations take elements from deductions as well as inferences. You're essentially making an inference about the material that you have, but in a way which involves deduction from the information rather than a loose conclusion based on what's most likely.

> <u>Let's recap the elements of interpretations:</u>
>
> Interpretations are careful evaluations of data;
>
> Interpretations don't deal with what's most likely in the same way inferences do, but rather they examine what logically follows from information given;
>
> This means that interpretations are often more reliable than inferences.

EVALUATING ARGUMENTS

Along with the four aforementioned skills that a critical thinker needs to possess, it's important to be able to evaluate arguments in a more general sense. Critical thinkers need to be able to figure out how strong an argument is by comparing it to the information it's based on.

This can be slightly more abstract than previous areas we've covered. For the critical techniques so far, the methods have been relatively straight-forward, with little room for ambiguity or debate. Here, what constitutes a strong or weak argument usually depends on

how relevant the argument is, how well-supported it is by the statement, and whether or not it avoids argumentative fallacies.

Informal Fallacies

We took a look at informal fallacies in chapter 2, but they're just as relevant here. Evaluation of arguments will usually involve spotting any fallacies that might be present in an argument that either yourself or someone else is making. Therefore, you should take some time to read all of the explanations for those arguments, as well as the examples given.

As a general rule, an argument is weak if it relies on an informal fallacy. For example, if an argument only works by making use of a slippery slope, then the argument is weak. Therefore, it's vital that you know what these fallacies are and that you can identify them in an argument.

While some fallacies are well-telegraphed and easy to spot in arguments, this isn't always the case. For example, one argument might include a slippery slope, and even explicitly state that there's the possibility of a slippery slope. For example:

> *'If we make euthanasia legal, this will put us on a slippery slope where eventually people feel that they have the <u>duty</u> to die once they get to a certain age, rather than just the <u>right</u> to die.'*

This is a slippery slope argument made explicit, and therefore is incredibly easy to identify. However, not all fallacies are as easily noticed. For example:

> **'If we make euthanasia legal, then what is currently the _right_ to die will become the _duty_ to die.'**

This is the same argument as the one made above, but without explicit reference to it being a slippery slope. A good way to identify the slippery slope is to see if the argument says that one thing could lead to another, without sufficient evidence to explain why. In particular, this change is suggested to be inevitable, and sets off a chain of events. However, some slippery slopes might cover this up by using the words 'could', or 'might' as opposed to terms which imply inevitability, such as 'will' or 'must'.

In this case, there's no evidence available to support the idea that gives individuals the right to die on their own terms would lead to individuals feeling that they had the duty to die because they believed themselves to be a burden. Therefore, the argument is stating that one event will lead to another without sufficient evidence.

However, slippery slopes aren't necessarily fallacious. If there is sufficient evidence for one event leading to another, then the slippery slope isn't a fallacious one. However, these cases often aren't referred to as slippery slopes.

One final thing to remember in general about logical fallacies is that, just because an argument contains a fallacy, it doesn't mean that the position that they're defending is incorrect. Rather, it just means that the argument presented, or even just the person who has presented it, is at fault. Someone could defend a completely legitimate position very poorly. For this reason, you shouldn't assume that an entire position is incorrect just because of the way it has been argued. Rather, the argumentation is at fault.

<u>To summarise the evaluation of arguments:</u>

- This critical technique is focused less on what method is used to derive the conclusion, but instead looks at the argumentative tools at play;

- Logical fallacies are the main thing to look out for when evaluating an argument, whilst also considering if the inferences, deductions, interpretations and assumptions being made are adequate;

Just because an argument contains a fallacy, that doesn't mean the position it's defending is incorrect. Rather, it just means that the argument presented is poor.

CONCLUSION

In this chapter, you've learned the five main critical techniques that you'll likely come across when reading critically and participating in discussions or debates. Now, let's turn our attention to writing critically. This will be the focus of the next chapter.

CRITICAL WRITING

Now that you've learnt how to think critically, it's time to think about how to write critically. Critical writing is vital for individuals in academic areas, such as students and researchers, since the skill of writing critically will aid you in forming your own arguments.

A mistake that many people make when writing essays is that they tend to only *describe* another point of view rather than *critique* it. Take a look at this example.

> In his essay 'Of the Standard of Taste', David Hume makes the argument that the way to determine which pieces of art are better than others is to establish a consensus from "true critics".

This is an adequate *description* of Hume's stance on taste, but for most essays this doesn't go far enough. On top of this, the writer needs to be prepared to apply *criticism*:

> In his essay 'Of the Standard of Taste', David Hume makes the argument that the way to determine which pieces of art are better than others is to establish a consensus from "true critics". **The issue with Hume's argument is that he doesn't give a subject-independent (i.e. objective) way to decide on who these "true critics" should be. Therefore, the decision on which art is "good" will be subjective.**

Here, we've added some critique to the passage to make it more robust. Now, we are challenging the viewpoint presented in the original passage. This is a form of criticism.

You can write critically about a piece of work in lots of different ways. Here are a few ideas:

- **Context** – examining the context of a piece is a good way to turn a passage from description into critique. Spend some time reading about the time period that the piece you are critiquing is from, and how that might have impacted the writer's point of view. For example, Thomas Hobbes lived through the chaos of the English Civil War, which might have informed his political beliefs.

- **Defining terms** – Taking a closer look at specific terms in detail is a way of thinking and writing in a critical manner. If a writer has used a term that is either vague or questionable, you should take a closer look at it!

- **Comparison** – Comparing two pieces of work is an excellent form of critique if you can pull it off. You need to be careful not to make your work too bloated by it, and you also need to be sure not to stray from the point. However, taking two competing ideas and pitting them against one another gives you room for critical analysis, as you point out similarities and

differences between them.

- **Counterarguments** – The most straight-forward and common way to write critically is to think of counterarguments to what you're writing about. You can start by finding some existing criticisms and paraphrasing them, and then add some thought of your own.

Let's look at each of these in more detail, starting with **context**.

CONTEXT

Context is a word used to describe the circumstances which have an impact on an idea or piece of work. Ideas don't exist in isolation, and since human beings are affected by their environments, so too are their ideas and works. For example, Cartesian scepticism inherently questions the very existence of everything around us, yet Descartes's argument is predicated on the notion that God exists. This seems like an inconsistency in his argument: that he would be so sceptical of the existence of *everything* except God.

However, it's important to consider the context of Descartes's argument. Living and writing in the 17th Century, he grew up in a deeply Christian society in which the highest levels of education were controlled by religious institutions. Therefore, Descartes was likely to hold some degree of religious belief. In turn, this might explain *why* he didn't question the existence of God during the opening chapters of *Meditations,* saving this discussion for *Meditation III*.

So, examining the context of Descartes's scepticism gives us some insight into *why* there's a degree of inconsistency in his perspective. While this doesn't mean we can't criticise this contradiction, it's something worth commenting on since it shows that you have a greater understanding of the landscape of the time he was writing in.

DEFINING TERMS

As previously mentioned, it's important to make sure that your understanding and usage of terms is razor-sharp when writing critically. Not only this, but you also need to be prepared to focus on vague terminology used by thinkers. If a concept has multiple possible meanings, highlight this in your argument – it'll show that you've considered the definitions of important ideas, and how misinterpretation could lead to drastically different results.

In addition, you should take a look at how different thinkers use the same terms when discussing the same issues. It may be the case that, while both writers are using the same terminology and arguing over the same problem, they're not quite speaking about the same thing. This could result in the two talking past one another rather than addressing each other's arguments.

For example, two writers might be discussing the rise in neo-fascist groups in Western society, and what has caused it. The term 'fascist' is notorious for being vague in meaning, as it has been applied to various ideologies, parties, governments, and groups across the political spectrum. One of the two participants might argue that neo-fascism is reserved for right-wing racist groups, whilst the other might define neo-fascism as *any* group with totalitarian and violent tendencies. Unless these two participants identify the differences in their meaning and account for them, they won't be talking about the same thing. This is something you could focus on in your own argument, perhaps explaining why the two aren't reaching any kind of resolution.

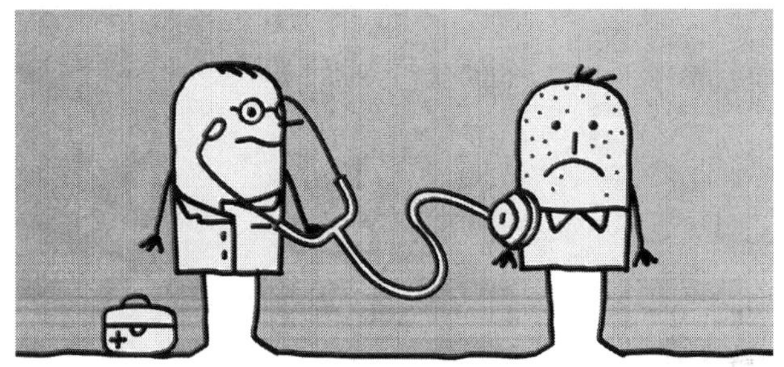

COMPARISON

The words of other people are often vital for criticising an argument, since you can call on the works of those with more experience than you. Comparing the ideas of two thinkers can expose flaws in both, giving you something to write critically about.

However, your argument can't be "Person *Y* thinks the opposite to Person *X*. Therefore, Person *Y* is wrong." You need to consider why one perspective is more reasonable than the other, rather than just pick a winner.

<u>Here are some questions to ask yourself about two competing perspectives:</u>

Which argument works better from a purely logical standpoint?

- Are these arguments talking about the same thing? Refer to your list of definitions to check;

- Does the criticism of one argument by the opposing participant get to the root of the problem?

- Does the participant providing the criticism give any solution themselves? If not, is this a problem?

COUNTERARGUMENTS

Ultimately, any method of being critical in your writing is going to come back to providing a counterargument. By counterargument, we simply mean providing a reason why an idea might be incorrect.

For example, one might argue that the reason why nature operates so smoothly is because there is an omnipotent and benevolent god controlling everything. The counterargument to this thesis might be that, while nature operates very well, it doesn't 'behave' in a way that implies benevolence. This is because natural selection is inherently violent and callous. Therefore, the view that God controls nature can be questioned.

Counterarguments are the basis for any kind of critical writing, and they should be used in conjunction with context, definitions of terms, and comparisons.

TIPS FOR WRITING CRITICALLY

Now that you have some ideas about what you can focus on when writing critically, you should be in a great position to make your next essay less *descriptive* and more *critical*. Here are some tips for making your essay as critical as possible.

Paraphrasing

When writing critical essays, you'll often need to refer to someone else's point of view. In these cases, it might feel appropriate to include a quote.

While this isn't terrible practice, the issue lies in the fact that you'll likely have to explain the quote that you've just written to show that you understand it. Instead, cut out the quote and head straight into paraphrasing it. Unless the exact wording of a statement is vital to its meaning (for example, a line from a Shakespeare play), you should try to write it in your words, and put your own explanation into the paraphrase. This way, you'll save space in your word count for more in-depth critique.

The other benefit of paraphrasing is that it will force you to learn what quotes and phrases mean, giving you a better chance of constructing strong criticism of them. Try paraphrasing in your next essay rather than quoting, and see how it works for you!

Keep Track of Key Terms

In many subjects, terminology is vital for a proper understanding. When thinking, reading, and writing critically, it's important that you know all of the key terms in play. A poor understanding of a phrase could lead to you completely misconstruing an argument, which in turn could completely ruin your criticism of it. When doing your initial reading for an essay, make a note of all the specialist terms that the writer uses, and get clear definitions for all of them. For those which have a vague meaning, keep note of this: you might be able to use that as part of your argument.

Once you have these terms written down with definitions, keep them in an easy-to-read location whenever you're doing reading or writing for the essay. That way, you can compare definitions between writers and thinkers. This will make it easier to "translate" the ideas of two different pieces of work, especially when lots of different terms are being used.

Be Precise

Precision is vital when writing critically. Make sure to focus on minute details if necessary, picking apart arguments to tell if they're valid or not. A close eye will allow you to spot issues in arguments that others have written, meaning that you have more to discuss when constructing your own argument.

By precision, we mean that you need to keep an eye on the details of an argument, rather than the vague strokes of it. This means you might have to do the following:

- Read the same page, paragraph, or sentence repeatedly until you fully understand it!

- Read companion pieces and secondary sources in order to get a deeper meaning out of the material;

- Write out entire arguments in your own words, then compare them to other summaries that you find in reputable sources.

Make use of Other Writers' Perspectives

When you start writing critically, you might be tempted to charge headlong into a piece of work, trying to pick it apart by yourself. While you need to be able to use your own head to critique work adequately, you should prepare to use the words of others when critiquing an argument. Make use of online resources to find journals containing arguments and criticisms that you can use as 'ammunition' for your own. This way, you'll be able to support your own viewpoints.

CONCLUSION

In this chapter, we've covered the following areas:

- The four main angles for critical writing: context, defining terms, comparisons, and counterarguments;

- Top tips for improving your critical writing skills, such as paraphrasing instead of quoting and being precise.

You should now have plenty of room to work with when participating in critical writing. Be sure to use these in conjunction with material from earlier chapters to consolidate your critical skills!

CONCLUSION

You've now reached the end of *Rapid Skills for Students: How to Be Critical.* By using this book, you've given yourself the skills necessary to think, read, and write critically — a huge bonus for students looking to up their game academically. If you're heading into academic essays or exams, bear the information in this book in mind whilst revising and planning your work.

A FEW FINAL WORDS...

Hopefully, you will feel far more confident in what you know as well as where you need to improve.

For any test, it is helpful to consider the following in mind...

The Three 'P's
1. Preparation. Preparation is key to passing any test; you won't be doing yourself any favours by not taking the time to prepare. Many fail their tests because they did not know what to expect or did not know what their own weaknesses were. Take the time to re-read any areas you may have struggled with. By doing this, you will become familiar with how you will perform on the day of the test.

2. Perseverance. If you set your sights on a goal and stick to it, you are more likely to succeed. Obstacles and setbacks are common when trying to achieve something great, and you shouldn't shy away from them. Instead, face the tougher parts of the test, even if you feel defeated. If you need to, take a break from your work to relax and then return with renewed vigour. If you fail the test, take the time to consider why you failed, gather your strength and try again.

3. Performance. How well you perform will be the result of your preparation and perseverance. Remember to relax when taking the test and try not to panic. Believe in your own abilities, practise as much as you can, and motivate yourself constantly. Nothing is gained without hard work and determination, and this applies to how you perform on the day of the test.

We wish you the best of luck in all of your future endeavours!

WANT TO IMPROVE LEARN EVEN MORE REVISION TRICKS?

CHECK OUT OUR OTHER REVISION GUIDES:

Achieve 100% Series

FOR MORE INFORMATION ON OUR REVISION GUIDES, PLEASE CHECK OUT THE FOLLOWING:

WWW.HOW2BECOME.COM

Created and Published By
How2Become.com
FAST-TRACK SUCCESS
SPEED
READING
RAPID STUDY SKILLS FOR STUDENTS
POCKETBOOK

Created and Published By
How2Become.com
FAST-TRACK SUCCESS
ESSENTIAL
WRITING
TIPS
RAPID STUDY SKILLS FOR STUDENTS
POCKETBOOK

Created and Published By
How2Become.com
FAST-TRACK SUCCESS
24-HOURS
TO A
FIRST-CLASS
ESSAY
RAPID STUDY SKILLS FOR STUDENTS
POCKETBOOK

Created and Published By
How2Become.com
FAST-TRACK SUCCESS
QUICK-FIRE
MATHS
RAPID STUDY SKILLS FOR STUDENTS
POCKETBOOK

Created and Published By
How2Become.com
FAST-TRACK SUCCESS
ACE YOUR
TIME
MANAGEMENT
RAPID STUDY SKILLS FOR STUDENTS
POCKETBOOK

Created and Published By
How2Become.com
FAST-TRACK SUCCESS
IMPROVING
YOUR
MEMORY
RAPID STUDY SKILLS FOR STUDENTS
POCKETBOOK

Created and Published By
How2Become.com
FAST-TRACK SUCCESS
CONSTRUCTING
YOUR
ARGUMENT
RAPID STUDY SKILLS FOR STUDENTS
POCKETBOOK

Created and Published By
How2Become.com
FAST-TRACK SUCCESS
HOW TO
STUDY WITH
DYSLEXIA
RAPID STUDY SKILLS FOR STUDENTS
POCKETBOOK

Created and Published By
How2Become.com
FAST-TRACK SUCCESS
UNIVERSITY
SURVIVAL
POCKETBOOK
RAPID STUDY SKILLS FOR STUDENTS
POCKETBOOK

Get Access To

FREE Psychometric Tests

www.PsychometricTestsOnline.co.uk

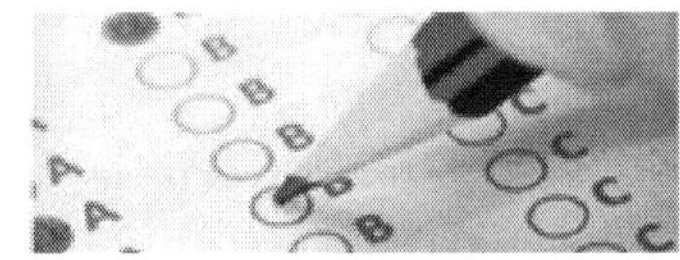

Printed and bound by CPI Group (UK) Ltd, Croydon, CR0 4YY

06/07/2026

02157570-0002